Teaching the Gifted and Talented in the English Classroom

by
William W. West

NEA's Teaching the Gifted and Talented
in the Content Areas series
Editor: Frederick B. Tuttle, Jr.

National Education Association
Washington, D.C.

Teaching the Gifted and Talented in the English Classroom

Note
The opinions expressed in this publication should not be
construed as representing the policy or position of the
National Education Association. Materials published as
part of this NEA multimedia program are intended to be
discussion documents for teachers who are concerned with
specialized interests of the profession.

Acknowledgment
The following material is reprinted with permission from
the source indicated: "The Faculty Club, Wittenberg" by
William Gavin from *English Journal*, January 1967; copy-
right © 1967 by the National Council of Teachers of
English.

Library of Congress Cataloging in Publication Data

West, William Walter, 1925-
    Teaching the gifted and talented in the English class-
      room.
    Bibliography: p.
    1. Gifted children—Education—Language arts.
2. Gifted children—Education—English language.
I. Title.
LC3993.27.W47   371.9'5   79–22396
ISBN 0-8106-0734-4

Contents

The Author

William W. West is Professor of English Education in the College of Education at the University of South Florida, Tampa.

The Advisory Panel

Dr. Natalie C. Apple, English teacher, Allderdice High School, Pittsburgh, Pennsylvania

Dr. Allen Berger, Professor of Language Communications, University of Pittsburgh, Pennsylvania

Bonnie S. Dibble, English teacher, Seminole High School, Seminole, Florida

Jeffrey N. Golub, teacher of English and Speech, Kent Junior High School, Kent, Washington

Isabelle M. Kamm, Chairperson, English Department, Wall Township High School, Wall, New Jersey

John B. Karls, Curriculum Specialist—English Language Arts, Milwaukee Public Schools

Dr. Patricia O. Tierney, English teacher, Allderdice High School, Pittsburgh, Pennsylvania

Gladys V. Veidemanis, Chairperson, English Department, North High School, Oshkosh, Wisconsin

The Series Editor

NEA's *Teaching the Gifted and Talented in the Content Areas* series Editor is Frederick B. Tuttle, Jr.

Dr. Tuttle is Associate Professor at the State University of New York, College at Brockport; Director of the Program for Gifted and Talented in the Foxborough Schools System, Massachusetts; and Consultant Boston College/Boston City Schools District 3 Gifted and Talented. Among his publications are *Composition: A Media Approach,* *Technical and Scientific Writing* (with Sarah H. Collins), and What Research Says to the Teacher: *Gifted and Talented Students,* published by NEA.

INTRODUCTION

The Faculty Club, Wittenberg

They say young Hamlet died. A pity, that.
So handsome, young, and rich. I fear his mind
Was never really on his books. He sat
Alone, rear of the room. You know the kind:
Not much to say in class; some days he'd mope
And pout and stare and never say a word.
He failed test after test, then dropped. No hope

Of passing me. They say he knew the sword
Quite well. I rarely find time to attend
The matches. A prince. To me, just one more
Young man with too much gold and time to spend,
The kind who whines that lectures are a bore.
Did thoughts disturb that sullen, noble head?
I never did find out. And now he's dead. (4)

One can readily picture the complacent professor, happily ensconced before a roaring fire at the club, hands folded across "fair belly with good capon lin'd," reminiscing about the death of a former student. In the professor's few self-satisfied words, one relives with Hamlet the endless low-level lectures, the monotonous droning insistence upon conformity, and the tragic lack of challenge of the gifted youth's school career:

Did thoughts disturb that noble, sullen head?
I never did find out. And now he's dead.

To borrow the words of the United Negro College Fund, "A mind is a terrible thing to waste!"

And the tragedy is intensified if the wasted mind—from any person, black or white, male or female, rich or poor, young or old—has the rare qualities of the gifted or potentially gifted. Lost, then, are both the gifted mind and the contributions which only such minds can offer.

The difference between the gifted and the potentially gifted becomes clear as one examines the behaviors of students. Gifted students are those who have developed (or are developing) at a higher level than most other students. Potentially gifted students are those who have latent abilities, but who have not—for personal, familial, subcultural,

9

social, or educational reasons—yet achieved sufficiently along culturally approved lines to merit the label "gifted."

English language arts teachers have a doubly important responsibility in identifying, developing, challenging, and rewarding the gifted. Language skill is not only frequently a marker of giftedness, but it is also a desirable goal in its own right. Moreover, it is the major vehicle both for the realization of giftedness in other areas and for the expression and communication of insights from all areas. Finally, only by using language skillfully can gifted individuals exert leadership and stimulate the "corporate creativity" which marks modern culture. When an English language arts teacher fails to develop language skills in a potentially gifted student, not only do the "English" fields of language, literature, composition, reading, and oracy suffer, but the entire spectrum of human endeavor misses opportunities. Perhaps it is not too sentimental to mourn with Thomas Gray that

Some mute inglorious Milton here may rest. . . .

Without the communication skills which only skillful language instruction can promote, the gifted necessarily remain either mute or less-than-realized, and giftedness in every area is frustrated.

CHARACTERISTICS OF THE GIFTED IN ENGLISH

A truism regarding teaching is that good teaching magnifies individual differences. Because good teaching enables students to achieve to the level of their abilities and because abilities differ, good teaching increases the spread among individuals. In much the same way, one can say that giftedness magnifies individual differences. Because few students are gifted in exactly the same ways and because their divergent gifts permit them to grow rapidly in different ways, the differences among them increase. Consequently it is difficult to characterize the gifted, either in English or in any other field. Equally gifted students will be quite different from each other.

Perhaps the one safe generalization regarding the gifted is that the gifted student is likely to adapt most rapidly and most successfully to the total environment. Consequently, whatever the culture, by adapting rapidly and successfully gifted students become ". . . almost invariably more popular and more socially accepted than children at other levels of intellectual ability." (3) By adapting quickly to responsive and receptive environments, such students become popular and accepted leaders.

On the other hand, some gifted students may be shy and withdrawn. The generalization just noted may also explain this quite different behavior. These children may also be "adapting rapidly and successfully," if nonresponsive and nonreceptive elements in their environment are encouraging a different type of adaptation. Perhaps mindless demands for conformity mandate withdrawal as the only way of preserving individuality. Perhaps well-intentioned, but frustrating, back-to-the-basics drills on previously mastered fundamentals make nonparticipation the only escape from boredom. Perhaps a subcultural value—such as the Pueblo Indians' shame at standing out from peers, or the embarrassment of some Blacks at being identified with the establishment—may generate various kinds of withdrawal, noncooperation, or independent action. These, too, are ways of "adapting rapidly and successfully" to the total environment.

IDENTIFYING STUDENTS GIFTED IN ENGLISH

Although former U.S. Commissioner of Education Ernest Boyer indicated that only approximately four percent of gifted students are receiving instruction in programs appropriate to their needs, many of the gifted reveal themselves at once. The gifted in English often manifest the following behaviors: they read avidly—though without guidance they often read less-than-challenging materials; they write fluently and frequently, often composing experimentally for their own pleasure; they enjoy participating in oral activities; and they perceive and produce humor and language play.

The potentially gifted, on the other hand, may possess latent but undisplayed abilities, so the teacher needs to use all possible sources of information to aid evaluation. Though not infallible, school records often provide insights beyond directly observable clues. By using cumulative and anecdotal records, reports on standardized group tests, creativity tests, individual IQ tests, behavior rating scales, and other evaluative measures, teachers may gain insights into undeveloped abilities. These sources, however, are no substitute for careful observation in locating such traits of the gifted which Guilford describes as "ideational fluency, associative fluency, and expressional fluency." (5)

In addition to noting obviously outstanding students and examining school records, teachers must very carefully observe all students including those who are disruptive, withdrawn, passive, and constantly conforming. They should attempt to evaluate their behaviors in terms of *their total environments,* insofar as is possible, in order to determine which students are adapting rapidly and successfully. Such observation will include individual conversations with the children, discussions of values and attitudes, experiments permitting self-selection of activities, and individualization of personal planning and record-keeping over a period of time. It will include attempts to learn about students' homes and families and subcultures and behaviors in nonschool settings. It will also include the designing of little "experiments," such as the use of word games, to assess skills sometimes hidden in formal academic situations. These types of observations are crucial, even as the teacher is making other direct judgments in terms of actual, observable language use.

In guiding observations of language behavior, the following kinds of questions are valuable:

Language

1. Is the student acquainted with and responsive to fluent, imaginative, creative, and colorful?
2. Does the student's language conform to the models respected in the subculture? (These may differ from standard classroom models!)
3. Is the student confident in expressing ideas in the familiar subcultural environment?

Literature

1. Is the student acquainted with and responsive to traditional literature of transescence and adolescence beyond the level of peers?

2. Is the student familiar with and responsive to varied materials from different periods, locations, and genres?
3. Has the student developed areas of special depth and interest?
4. Does the student enjoy listening to and watching literary performances?

Composition

1. Has the student developed the basic mechanical skills which provide freedom and confidence for additional growth? ("Perfection" would not be a requisite for a favorable response to this question.)
2. Does the student make and support observations and opinions beyond the capacity of peers?
3. Does the student write independently? (Diaries, journals, imaginative writing)
4. Does the student respect writing and choose to engage in it for various purposes?

Reading

1. Is the student confident of word analysis, phonics, vocabulary from context, and other skills?
2. Does the student have listening, reading, writing, and speaking vocabularies beyond those of peers?
3. Does the student possess abilities in comprehension, interpretation, evaluation, and rate beyond those of peers?
4. Does the student have independent study, library, dictionary, and research skills?

Oracy

1. Is the student confident in initiating purposeful conversations with peers, adults, strangers?
2. Does the student enjoy participating in discussions and conversations, and in delivering brief announcements and literary selections?
3. Is the student comfortable with the courtesies and conventions of social intercourse?
4. Does the student use and appreciate humor in speech?

Special Interests

1. Does the student work independently, persistently, over a period of time on individually chosen personal projects?
2. Does the student seek details of and applications for self-chosen areas of interest?

Activities to Determine Student Abilities

The foregoing questions should assist teachers either in recommending students for specialized programs or in meeting the needs of the gifted within a self-contained classroom. In addition, student skills associated with giftedness may also be determined through some interesting, informal activities. Here, for example, are a few fun activities usable at almost every level to gain insights into student abilities.

Verbal fluency

Tell students you will give them the name of one letter of the alphabet. In three minutes they are to list all words beginning with that letter, exclusive of inflectional and derivational variants (singular and plural of nouns, and library, librarian, for example). Allowing for occasional psychological blocks and other inhibitory problems, the length of individual lists roughly indicates verbal fluency.

Originality

Tell students you will give them the name of a common object. In three minutes they are to list all possible uses of a single such object, using their imaginations to conceive of possibilities rarely actually employed. Then give them the name of such an object as a single brick, a single paper clip, a single sheet of paper, a single fork, or a single toothpick. After exhausting obvious uses, more imaginative students will expand possibilities either by transforming their observer point of view (a brick, for example, might do for a mouse to hide behind, or a toothpick might be a javelin for a cricket) or by transforming the physical state of the object (a crushed and powdered brick might be used either as an abrasive for sandpaper or as the pigment in lipstick). Again, the length of the lists correlates roughly with originality, although this ability changes with practice.

Ability to elaborate

Give students a single, unusual, and perhaps connotatively directional name. Have them imagine and list the physical and psychological characteristics of a person with that name (Martin Chuzzlewit, Marjorie Morningstar, Uriah Heep, Hester Prynne). Whether names are imaginary or derived from literature, a student's ability to elaborate should be judged strictly in terms of length and internal consistency of the list, rather than in terms of accuracy or "correctness."

Ability to synthesize

Give students the names of from three to five quite different and unrelated objects (a ring, a small Japanese dictionary, a matchstick, a Phillips screw, and a fragment of tapestry; a seashell, a light bulb, a fragment of road map, a piece of agate, and a child's block). In three minutes, each child is to create a story explaining the presence of individual items and the connections among them. You may provide a setting, or context, for the items. ("These were found in the pockets of a spy." "This collection was in the desk of a woman who mysteriously disappeared.") Younger children may tell their stories; older children may write theirs. If students are to write their stories—which you may have them do after they have shared by telling their ideas—they will require a good deal longer time. Ability to synthesize is evident from the degree to which the presence and connection of the objects is clear and natural.

Flexibility

Give students one or more short quotations, such as "Now is the time for all good people to come to the aid of the party." or "Give me liberty or give me death." In a certain period, students are to create complete, natural, and meaningful sentences (one or more) using the successive letters in each quotation as the first letters in successive words. (For example, the beginning of *Now is the time* . . . might stimulate the words "*N*ext *O*ctober *w*e *i*ntend *s*ending *T*om *h*elp *e*ach *t*ime *i*n *m*inor *e*mergencies. . . .") Determine students flexibility from the length, sense, and well-formed nature of their sentences.

Ability to reach closure

Give students single-picture cartoons from which laugh lines or captions have been deleted, and ask them to suggest appropriate labels. Have students supply missing final lines to couplets, quatrains, or limericks. Have students suggest possible resolutions, or steps to produce resolution, for conflicts from newspaper stories, literature, or experience. Determine ability to reach closure from the simplicity, propriety, consistency, and probable effect of their suggestions.

The professional judgment of individual teachers should probably be primary in the location of gifted students for special classes—and will certainly be primary in determining who receives special experiences within the self-contained classroom. Nonetheless, biographical inventories prepared by students, as well as student, parent, and peer recommendations should also be considered.

These, then, are some techniques for locating and selecting gifted and potentially gifted students in the English language arts:

1. Use all the data-collection resources of the school system contained in cumulative and anecdotal records, including standardized group tests, creativity tests, individual IQ tests, behavior rating scales, and other institutionalized evaluative measures.

2. Observe individual students and interpret their verbal behavior in terms of their total environment—insofar as it is possible to do so.

3. Supplement your observations over a period of time with brief, focused fun activities which reveal attributes of the gifted.

One especially important *caveat* for teachers attempting to locate gifted students is that greatness lies not in freedom from faults, but in abundance of powers. Few teachers today would equate "correctness" in language usage with giftedness; it is equally to be desired that few teachers would reject gifted students whose language may not be considered conventionally "correct."

ENGLISH LANGUAGE ARTS ACTIVITIES FOR THE GIFTED

Two recent studies of the composition and literature objectives of the well-established gifted program in the city of Pittsburgh list thirty different "Strategies for Teaching Scholars English." (1,6) A quick look at the list readily reveals that the activities utilized in teaching the gifted Pittsburgh scholars are not significantly different from the kinds of activities utilized in teaching all students. Perhaps the same would be said of most gifted programs everywhere. Included in the Pittsburgh list are the following:

1. Teacher lecture
2. Class discussion
3. Small group discussion
4. Study guides
5. Reading quiz
6. Objective examination
7. Essay examination
8. Oral report by individuals
9. Panel discussion
10. Independent project by individuals
11. Independent project by a group
12. Outside speaker
13. Audiovisual aid
14. Games
15. Contracts
16. Sensory exercises
17. Role-playing
18. Pantomime
19. Performance of a play
20. Vocabulary enrichment exercises
21. Single paragraph exposition
22. Multiparagraph exposition
23. Comparison and contrast paper
24. Opinion paper
25. Book report
26. Descriptive paragraph
27. Narrative writing
28. Poetry writing
29. Research paper
30. Speech

Though extensive but not exhaustive, the list requires an environment, or setting, including a kind of philosophy for the teaching of language to the gifted in order to give it life and meaning. Perhaps a good place to begin is with John Dewey's classic statement:

> Think of the absurdity of having to teach language as a thing by itself. If there is anything the child will do before he goes to school, it is to talk of the things that interest him. But when there are no vital interests

appealed to in the school, when language is used simply for the repetition of lessons, it is not surprising that one of the chief difficulties of school work has come to be instruction in the mother-tongue. Since the language taught is unnatural, not growing out of the real desire to communicate vital impressions and convictions, the freedom of children in its use gradually disappears, until finally the high school teacher has to invent all kinds of devices to assist in getting any spontaneous and full use of speech. Moreover, when the language instinct is appealed to in a social way, there is a continual contact with reality. The result is that the child always has something in his mind to talk about, he has something to say; he has a thought to express, and a thought is not a thought unless it is one's own. In the traditional method, the child must say something that he has merely learned. There is all the difference in the world between having something to say and having to say something. (2)

With Dewey's *caveat* in mind, then, we need some kind of construct to enable us to *splice* all the elements of a creative language arts program into one seamless golden garment suitable for the teaching of the gifted. Perhaps the mnemonic acronym SPLICE-P$_3$ will guide recall of the elements of such a program.

> S—The *subject* matter of such a program will be *significant* and often *student-selected*. One of the tragic and self-defeating problems of a "back-to-basics" program is that—as important as capitalization, punctuation, and spelling are to the acceptance of a communication and a communicator—in isolation each element remains trivial and inconsequential rather than significant. Effective teachers have long been aware that for many students the worst way of teaching the basics is to teach these skills directly. The teacher of the gifted will look first for *significant, sometimes student-selected and student-created subject matter* and—when necessary—guide the improvement of basic skills within the context of purposeful communication.

18

P—Subject matter alone is not enough. Without *purpose* or *plan* the field lies inert, unmoving, and unchallenging. Admittedly, graduate scholars are motivated to know all about a field to which they have committed their lives, whether or not there is any foreseeable purpose in mastering all the dialects of the Ashkenazi or plotting the migrations of the Kurds in the twelfth century. But for immature adolescents, bombarded every moment by challenges and stimuli from competing areas of interest, life is too short to devote to purposeless activity. The teacher of the gifted will quickly *plan* some *purpose* for concentration of effort on a given subject. Often that *plan* or *purpose* includes the solving of a *problem*.

L—If *The Republic* is ever to realize Socrates' (and Plato's) vision of rule by the wisest, the gifted must be trained in *leadership*. Although there are many kinds of leadership and many leaders who are not "gifted" in the academic, verbal sense, significant language arts activities must include opportunities to develop and exercise *leadership* abilities. In the first place, the language arts are by definition social, cooperative, and concerned with communication, and when students are placed in cooperative social settings involving purposeful communication, *leadership* emerges and *leadership* skills develop. Wise teachers begin with institutional leadership by appointing chairs and captains, but they train students to select democratic leaders, and they search for the rare and dramatic charismatic leaders for whom pivotal historic moments wait.

I—In solving significant problems, student leaders will not be restricted by the limitations of the teacher or the subject matter. Consequently, many studies will be, in part, *independent* and *interdisciplinary*. When uniform in-class activity is productive, the teacher will not hesitate to use all the traditional tools of pedagogy, including lecture and drill, but since the essence of language development is *independent* and purposeful language generation, effective teachers know when to devote class time to *independent* and small group activity and how to stimulate out-of-class production. Likewise, since language permeates all disciplines, and since "English" has no monopoly on the stimulation of language, wise teachers borrow from all relevant disciplines. Activities will be partly *independent* and *interdisciplinary*.

C—*Creating* according to Webster, is the "bringing into existence, or the producing, or the investing with a new form" of some thing or idea. Such *creating* is especially relevant to programs for the gifted since *creation* and *creativity* are attributes of the gifted as well as goals of gifted programs. Often, units of study will have as their end the experience of *creativity* and the actual *creation* of diverse and original projects.

E—A major characteristic of productive and creative cooperative effort is the generation of *energy* and the *extension* of powers and projects. In short, as in rhetorical synecdoche, the energy of a group is a whole that somehow becomes much greater than the sum of its parts. Sometimes called "synergy," this *extension* and generation of *energy* from group effort both simplifies and complicates the teaching of language arts to the gifted. Most educators have experienced instruction in which the instructor did most of the work, so that many sessions began with the lonely, difficult, and pitiable effort of teachers seeming to raise themselves and their entire class, without help, to the level of production. Language arts classes for the gifted when they generate synergy—*energy* and *extension*—lift themselves daily into productivity, move automatically from project to project, and inspire with a contagious vibrance the visitor can feel. The teacher may sometimes have difficulty channeling and controlling the synergy of such a class, but how preferable it is to the deadweight albatross of a listless group.

It becomes clear, then, from the SPLICE part of the acronym, that projects in the teaching of language arts to the gifted rarely are one-shot, one-period gimmicks to interest and inspire. Rather, significant learning emerges over a period of time as a *group* attacks a project or problem—at the same time individuals use it as a point of departure for their individual pursuits and processes.

And that brings us to the final element of the SPLICE-P_3 formula:

> P—The *product* is the terminal achievement of the SPLICE procedures. It is the outward and visible manifestation of the inward and invisible growth of the individuals during the series of lessons. In most cases, the *products* of language arts units also begin with the letter *P*: they are *performances* (plays, pantomimes, poetry readings), *publications* (newspapers, magazines, books, reports, anthologies), and *productions* (models, drawings, paintings, catalogs, inventions, machines). Their cooperative creation involves the constant purposeful creative use of language, and their demonstration and display elicit additional language. Their critique, revision, and improvement generate even more language.

DESIGN FOR A LESSON SEQUENCE

Whether preparing lessons for sixth or twelfth graders, the unit design is the same. Indeed, even the same subject matter, adapted to varying maturity and materials, can be used with several grades. Note that for development, extension, and involvement, most lesson sequences must extend over a period of several days. Also note that sometimes such lessons are *not* the exclusive concern of a class during a given period; rather, such lessons may coexist with numbers of other ongoing concerns so that the teacher, rather like a juggler, maintains interest by handling a number of subjects at the same time.

Interest Arousers

Regardless of age, maturity, degree of giftedness, or level of sophistication, students must be directed toward, focused on, and interested in a subject, topic, area, or problem. Many teachers build interest in a subject slowly over a period of time. Others pounce immediately on serendipitous events, programs, news items, or fads. Still others carefully schedule literature, films, speakers, recordings, videotapes, student performances, field trips, and other high-interest experiences to initiate concern for a subject. In most cases, these techniques require a degree of preparation: explanation of concepts, history, vocabulary, significance, and connection with prior experience.

Oral Language

Classical rhetoricians were trained to ask automatically a series of questions on any subject they were given. In this way, they learned to discover what Aristotle termed "all of the available means of persuasion." Although American students are given no such formal training in looking at subjects, yet in the natural give and take of exploratory discussion—questioning and responding, relating, comparing, contrasting, analyzing, and so on—they automatically ask and answer many of the questions rhetoricians took such pains to learn. By doing so, they explore the significance of a subject, investigate causes and effects, perceive possibilities, make connections, observe details, and generate interest. In addition to being good practice in thinking and in using language, this step is essential is getting students to develop an emotional connection with unit subjects.

Group Planning

Although the teacher does a great deal of preplanning (collecting materials, organizing concepts, allocating time, scheduling events, and so on), letting students help enriches and enlivens subsequent lessons. Tasks they initiate, groups they form, responsibilities they plan—all are much more meaningful and rewarding than arbitrary teacher-imposed assignments. Some groups can handle such planning easily; some must be taught to do so. Let each class handle all the responsibility it is capable of.

Research and Creative Activity

This step changes the gifted classroom from the learn-and-recite, the assignment-correction paradigm. The teacher allows class time for individual and group research and production. Nonetheless, this step cannot be restricted to the limitations of the class period and the class room. Viewed differently from "homework," individuals and groups act purposefully in moving toward closure on their projects.

Performance, Presentation, or Production

Although the "P" stage is the last element of the SPLICE-P$_3$ system, it is the next-to-the-last element during the actual teaching sequence. The basic purpose of language is communication, and purposeful communication is such a strong stimulant of language that with the goal of performance, publication, or production clearly specified and scheduled, students are strongly stimulated to use language well. And the performance, presentation, and production generate still more language experience in yet another step.

Discussion and Critique (and possible revision)

This final stage involves all the thinking processes at the upper level of Bloom's taxonomy: *analysis* of meanings, methods, implications, ideas in the "P" step; *synthesis* of ideas from several different productions or approaches; *evaluation* of performances, publications, or productions. This "student reaction" step provides both reward and motivation at the same time it stimulates additional understanding of concepts and improvement of process and products.

Students become aware of the importance of and opportunities for polishing and perfecting, but teacher and class may decide in many cases not to revise specific projects. They determine whether such a revision and the learning it will stimulate are worth the additional effort.

AN EXAMPLE OF A TEACHING SEQUENCE

The lesson sequence just explored is especially productive if used with gifted classes, but it is also flexible enough for heterogeneous classes including gifted students. Indeed, the fact that gifted students have an opportunity to work with and lead other students is sometimes an added value.

Here is how such a teaching sequence might evolve.

I. Interest Arouser
   A. Over a period of time, the teacher has referred to miscellaneous examples of unexplained phenomena: the yeti in the Himalayas; the mysterious footsteps leading to every house in Devonshire, England, in 1855; the reports of flying saucers; reports of poltergeists. At odd moments, the class discusses these and other events. The teacher promises vaguely "sometime" to play the recording of Orson Welles's 1938 broadcast "The War of the Worlds."
   B. One day, with a minimum of preparation, the teacher plays the famous Welles record.
   C. With the help of the librarian, the teacher displays on a book truck in class a whole rack of whatever in the school is available on mystery, magic, science fiction, legend, and witchcraft.

II. Oral Language
   A. By laying the groundwork in advance and spending little time introducing the record before playing it, the teacher reserves time immediately following the record for oral language about it. The discussion is freewheeling and unstructured; yet the participating students cover the basic critical questions of literature: (1) What was the author-producer saying? (2) How was it said? (3) How well was it said? (4) Was it worth saying? In addition, they go beyond the "text" to discuss their own prior experiences with space and science fiction, their hypotheses regarding why the program was powerful, and their projections regarding space, space-travel, and the existence of life beyond earth. They may also discuss the original effect of the production, in the context of the times, and their interpretations of the shape similar programs today might take.
   B. Both the teacher and an official "scribe" keep notes during the discussion, trying to preserve ideas for investigations, projects, creative writing, and other extension of the unit theme.

III. Group Planning

A. The next day, after a cursory read-back of the teacher's and scribe's notes, students list on the chalkboard or overhead projector ideas and projects worth pursuing. Noted as questions, topics, hypotheses, projects, or assertions, these ideas are in no particular grammatical form and can be freely changed in any number of ways. A typical list might include such ideas as these:

1. Who was H. G. Wells and what else did he write?
2. Who was Orson Welles? What is he doing now?
3. What are some of the things that happened as a result of the broadcast? What has been written about it?
4. What was going on in the world about the time of Welles's broadcast?
5. Why were people so nervous and so willing to be panicked?
6. What do scientists now believe about life in outer space?
7. What is the current status of flying saucer research?
8. What have the Mars and Venus and Jupiter space probes revealed?
9. What would happen if something similar to "The War of the Worlds" were broadcast today?
10. What equivalent kind of broadcast on what kind of subject might cause a panic today?
11. Display? Pictures? Paintings? Creatures?
12. Models of space ships? Satellite station?
13. Poems about space?
14. Science fiction available in our library?
15. Interview program with "survivors" of Martian invasion? Types of people? Reactions?
16. Humorous events? One-act play, comedy, on humorous events?

17. Newspaper front page or original articles based on invasion?
18. Original radio play for modern audience? TV play?
19. Original short story or narrative? Experimentation with point of view (perhaps a Martian tells a story and sees humor or irony in things we take for granted)?
20. Description of creatures by us; description of us by creatures?

B. Either in class as a whole, or in small groups, students select clusters of ideas and brainstorm to develop them further. Students suggest sources of information when they can do so. (For example, for item 7—current status of flying saucer research—one student may suggest the library card catalog, a recent encyclopedia, recent issues of *Smithsonian* magazine, the *Reader's Guide to Periodical Literature,* the name of a local flying saucer buff who might either provide information or agree to appear as a speaker.) They also suggest actual development of certain ideas. (For item 18—original radio play for modern audience—they might suggest an impending China syndrome disaster in a nuclear power plant or a complete energy embargo.)

C. In a return to whole-class discussion, the teacher helps guide and schedule class activities so that individuals and groups can plan their work. Some guidance includes the following:
1. Acquainting students with resources unfamiliar to them, such as
   a. *Reader's Guide to Periodical Literature*
   b. Vertical file
   c. Annual yearbooks of certain encyclopedias (to help students determine events contemporary with the 1938 broadcast)
   d. Annual chronologies in the *World Almanac and Book of Facts* and *Information Please Almanac*

26

e. *Current Biography* (for information on Orson Welles and other figures)
f. *Dictionary of American Biography* for Americans, *Dictionary of National Biography* for information on H. G. Wells and other British figures
g. Special relevant Dewey decimal system numbers appropriate to the subject under consideration
h. Use of newspaper indexes, if appropriate
i. Availability of materials from the local newspaper archives (must, of course, be checked in advance)
j. Use of such special subject indexes as Granger's *Index to Poetry and Recitations, Bartlett's Familiar Quotations, Encyclopedia of Social Sciences,* and *Van Nostrand's Scientific Encyclopedia*

2. Informing students of the general uniform class activity schedule for reading and writing over the next several days.
3. Indicating class time available for reading, writing, group work, and group presentations.
4. Scheduling of any special films, recordings, or events related to the current theme. For example, the 56-minute color film *1985* is a fictionalized newscast produced by professional television newscasters describing the devastation of the modern world as pollution and complexity overwhelm contemporary civilization.
5. Students discuss various projects, eliminating some, expanding others, and gradually selecting certain ones to work on either individually or in different-sized groups.

IV. Research and Creative Activity
A. Because all groups must have common experiences to develop as groups, the teacher provides ongoing common experiences during this incubation and development period.

B. Knowing both class time available and due dates for presentations, students work both in class and outside class on their projects.

C. At regularly scheduled intervals, the teacher brings additional materials to class, acquaints students with other resources, calls for progress reports, and permits sharing of progress and problems.

V. Performance, Presentation, or Production

A. The individuals and groups present and explain their various creations. When effort and attainment justify wider audiences, they invite other classes, circulate publications beyond the class, and arrange displays in the library, study hall, central corridor, or other common areas.

B. While all students remain responsible for listening to and reacting to all presentations, certain individuals have primary responsibility both for rewarding and critiquing certain productions. They are taught, if necessary, that their evaluations must be diplomatic, clear, incisive, and well supported. They know all generalizations are subject to challenge and revision.

C. When possible, teachers save representative projects for future display and example. They see that suggestions for improvements are either realized or recorded.

VI. Discussion and Critique

Discussion and criticism involve personal, peer, and teacher evaluation, some of which is best handled in personal conference. Students critique themselves and their projects, indicating in writing time and effort spent on their projects, degree of commitment to the enterprise, special problems encountered, and judgment of the value of the project and the worth of the experience. When possible, they list suggestions for revision or improvement or changes in procedures.

Two or more peers also evaluate each project, reacting in writing to what the creators have presented. Evaluations are made independently but students later share impressions and resolve differences.

The teacher makes an independent evaluation and then, when possible, shares impressions with the evaluating team. Whenever possible, results are discussed in conference with each student.

SUGGESTIONS FOR SELECTING UNIT THEMES

Unlike schools and textbooks, the communications media must interest the public in order to exist. Consequently, editors, publishers, and producers have a pretty good idea of what will "sell." The teacher can do worse than to adapt editors' and producers' insights to the needs of education, recognizing of course that of "human interests" to which media cater, educational priorities always take precedence over mere interest. One communications list includes conflict, progress, importance, people, age (young or old), animals, mystery, sex, personal significance, and the unusual. Because students are likely to be interested in the same human interest subjects as adults, an easy way for the teacher to proceed is to search the media constantly over a long period of time and maintain files of topics and materials for class extension. Virtually all subjects about which individuals become emotionally involved can serve as stimulators to develop language, and though a single article will probably not provide sufficient raw material for research, development, and production, a collection of such articles can certainly do so.

English teachers are especially fortunate in that they have both the *methods* and *materials* of literature as resources. Because literature by definition is concerned with emotion, literary materials properly handled are more appealing to students and touch them more quickly than non-literary selections. Even when treating essentially "non-literary" materials—such as the content of science and social science—English instruction transmutes the material with a personal and emotional approach. Thus, the English teacher cares less about whether Balboa or Cortez "discovered" the

Pacific than about how the explorer felt as

> He star'd at the Pacific—and all his men
> Look'd at each other with a wild surmise—
> Silent, upon a peak in Darien.

This emotional approach of English even with "non-English" subject matter often allows students to relate rapidly and deeply to all content, even that from other disciplines.

SOME ACTIVITIES TO DEVELOP UPPER-LEVEL SKILLS

Although devising separate isolated activities to develop upper-level skills on Bloom's taxonomy is probably not a good idea, such activities inevitably emerge from a teaching sequence similar to that just discussed. The following list suggests ways in which these activities might emerge from a number of such units.

Analysis Skills

Student behaviors in this category involve the ability to break down and describe the components of an item and the relationships those components have to each other and to the whole. (See *Program Design and Development for Gifted and Talented Students* (7), p. 40.)

1. Sixth graders involved in a unit entitled "What Is a City?" define the functions of a city and analyze these functions into various components before beginning to plan and build a model city of their own.

2. Seventh graders, disturbed by the slaughter of whales on the high seas, seals in Canada, and dolphins off the coast of Japan, analyze reasons people war against nature. They then attempt to synthesize effective appeals to the people involved and to suggest alternative actions.

3. Eighth graders preparing individual vocations pamphlets as part of a "Personal Futures" unit analyze the

desirable careers projections of the U.S. Office of Manpower Division and contrast them with a similar analysis of current local opportunities as revealed in help wanted ads.

4. Ninth graders in a myth and folklore unit classify the themes of various selections in an attempt to understand and define the major types of traditional stories and their appeals to primitive peoples.

5. Tenth graders studying humor and satire collect contemporary examples to classify and analyze as to subject and appeal.

6. Eleventh graders studying *Macbeth* each take a character from the play and list and exemplify ways in which Shakespeare develops that character. Students then synthesize the results of their individual research to provide a relatively comprehensive analysis of the development of each character in *Macbeth*.

7. Twelfth graders studying modern written communications collect examples of kinds of business communications both from local businesses and from library models. They classify them as to types and then analyze and specify the characteristics of each type in a volume to be added to the library's permanent reference collection.

Synthesis Skills

This level of cognitive behavior requires ability to draw together ideas or materials from different sources to create something new. (See *Program Design and Development for Gifted and Talented Students* (7), p. 40.)

1. Sixth graders in a creative writing unit experiment with descriptive writing by specifying moods for various types of stories, embodying those moods in appropriate directional sentences; by listing various details which would contribute to those moods; and then by writing one or more descriptive paragraphs to capture and communicate such a mood without directly stating it.

They follow a similar procedure to develop characters for their stories, utilizing description, words, actions, symbols, and reports to communicate and support character.

2. Seventh graders studying television keep a diary of their viewing for about two weeks. From the details they have recorded, they generalize regarding their tastes and habits. Also, they synthesize their findings regarding various channels, networks, advertisers, and programs.

3. Eighth graders examining legends, superstitions, and folkways collect a large number of such beliefs, prepare a questionnaire, administer it to people near the school, and infer conclusions regarding contemporary beliefs.

4. Ninth graders entering the college preparatory program write a number of letters regarding entrance requirements to admissions officers of colleges to which they aspire. They then synthesize a list of requirements, including recommended high school courses.

5. Tenth graders studying biography and collective biography prepare lists of attributes, handicaps, areas of excellence, and foibles of various subjects whom they individually investigate. They then prepare some generalizations regarding these people and their achievements.

6. Eleventh graders investigating "Contributions of Science to Modern Thought" read independently in the history of science, in the biographies of scientists, and in the development of scientific thought. In addition, they interview scientists and teachers of science in an attempt to describe specific steps in a number of important scientific developments and to synthesize a description of the scientific method(s).

7. Twelfth graders, having each selected a different Nobel Prize winning author, read a minimum of three books by that author and prepare an essay attempting to define the author's style and values.

Evaluation Skills

Behaviors in this category involve judgments about value, purpose, or quality of an idea or item. (See *Program Design and Development for Gifted and Talented Students* (7), p. 40.)

1. Sixth graders each select two different Newbery Medal authors and read two books by each author. They then prepare an essay indicating which author they prefer, specifying reasons for their choices.

2. Seventh graders introduced to *Current Biography* select two figures from a field of their choice, read the entries carefully, supplement the information with additional research, and indicate which figure has so far made the greater contribution to that field and why.

3. Eighth graders reading collective biographies take limited notes on the entries about people in similar fields from such books as John Durant's *The Heavyweight Champions* (Hastings, 1975), Donald McCormick's *The Master Book of Spies* (Watts, 1974), or Milton J. Shapiro's *The Pro Quarterbacks* (Messner, 1971). Each student then selects a favorite person and prepares a report specifying the favorite and explaining and justifying the choice.

4. Ninth graders in a journalism unit obtain from the exchange editor of their school newspaper examples of student newspapers from twenty different schools. Each student reads several newspapers carefully, works out a set of specifications as to what makes a school newspaper effective, and then selects a favorite and explains and justifies the choice.

5. Tenth graders in a unit on "Problems and Young People" collect a number of Ann Landers or Dear Abby columns over several weeks. By classifying both the kinds of questions and the kinds of answers, they prepare to render a judgment as to the types of questions most commonly asked and the value of the answers.

6. Eleventh graders in a journalism unit have discussed and developed a set of standards for daily newspapers. Working in teams, they examine five or six issues each of three or four different large-city newspapers available in the school library. By tracing the evolution of three or four stories over several days in each of the newspapers, they prepare to evaluate each newspaper, to indicate their preference, and to justify their choice.

7. Twelfth graders in a careers unit obtain all the help possible from the guidance department, library, industry, and interviews to compile information regarding three possible careers for themselves. They then analyze their own interests and abilities and evaluate the three careers in terms of what they know about themselves.

Problem-Finding and Problem-Solving Skills

In working on solutions to problems, students may find it profitable to follow a general procedure such as the following:

- Identify a problem, focusing attention on specific aspects of a question or situation, especially questions that should be answered.
- Identify alternative solutions, brainstorming many ways of overcoming the problem and answering the necessary questions.
- Evaluate the alternatives, exploring positive and negative aspects of each alternative.
- Select the best alternative, realizing that this selection may be revised as new information is located.
- Try the alternative selected, evaluating its usefulness in solving the problem.
- Recycle the alternative selected, reassessing the legitimacy of the selection as it progresses through the steps. (See *Program Design and Development for Gifted and Talented Students* (7), pp 32–33.)

This is a general procedure for problem solving and will of course have to be modified according to the specific problem-solving situation.

1. Sixth graders listen daily in class either to a local radio news broadcast or a tape-recorded reproduction of such a broadcast. Each student keeps a diary of local concerns, and the entire class explores with adults and peers the nature and significance of local problems. Individuals and groups prepare letters to the editor on subjects about which they can take an intelligent stand or reach meaningful conclusions.

2. Seventh graders, after reading a number of books on contemporary life, including such books as Jean-Pierre Abraham's *The Pigeon Man* (Quist, 1971), Nan Hayden Agle's *Baney's Lake* (Seabury, 1972), *Go Ask Alice* (Prentice-Hall, 1971), Dorothy E. Shuttlesworth and Thomas Cervasio's *An Ecology Story: Litter, the Ugly Enemy* (Doubleday, 1973), each select a contemporary problem, do research, and prepare a report.

3. Eighth graders record and discuss problems mentioned in the city newspaper's letters to the editor and troubleshooter columns over a period of several weeks. Each then selects a problem to research and report on.

4. Ninth graders working on a unit on "My School and Myself" devise a questionnaire regarding school and school improvement to administer to teachers, upperclass students, and selected community members. From the results they select certain specific problems, prepare programs for improvement of these problems, and evaluate the success of the programs.

5. Tenth graders in a required social studies course on "Problems of American Democracy" coordinate a term paper unit with assignments in the English department so that each student treats in depth with traditional academic apparatus a library resources paper on a selected problem.

6. Eleventh graders keep logs over a four-week period of contemporary problems handled on such programs as "Lou Grant," "All in the Family," "One Day at a Time,"

and "Sixty Minutes." They then prepare a brief introduction to a paper by summarizing the attitude or solution the programs seem to suggest, continuing with a researched analysis of the problem from library sources, and concluding with an evaluation of the program's treatment of the problem.

7. Twelfth graders procure, duplicate, and discuss copies of the most recent Common Cause Citizen's Lobby questionnaire. They rank-order the problems as to importance, compare their conclusions with those of adults to whom they administer a questionnaire, and then prepare reports to send both to Common Cause and to legislators. Individuals and groups select specific problems on which to do library research.

Creative Thinking Skills

Creative thinking, essentially, is the kind of thinking which permits the combination of previously acquired knowledge and skills into new and original arrangements and patterns.

1. Sixth graders, having read or listened to such stories as *Swiss Family Robinson, Robinson Crusoe,* "Robinson Crusoe's Island" by Charles E. Carryl, "If Once You've Slept on an Island" by Rachel Field, and having heard about such stories as Shakespeare's *Tempest,* Golding's *Lord of the Flies,* and James Barrie's *Admirable Crichton,* spend time daily in imagining, discussing, developing, and recording life shipwrecked on an isolated island. They create a society, develop a set of laws and customs, and plan a village.

2. Seventh graders studying the geography and history of the United States plan and take, in imagination, a yearlong trip around the country. They determine how far they can travel each day, where they want to go, what they want to see, and what they will do. As the trip gets under way, various students research, create, report on, and record the sights and activities at each stop, as well as the historical significance for the specific locations.

3. Eighth graders studying the westward movement in America have read or heard James Daugherty's *Of Courage Undaunted* or Julia Davis's *No Other White Men,* both stories of the Lewis and Clark Expedition. They begin to keep a daily journal of the trip, describing adventures they have, country they see, and flora and fauna they collect. They plot the trip on a large map and arrange continuing displays of both art work and creative writing, as well as commercial materials.

4. Ninth graders studying "Coming of Age" and "Problems of Young People" read widely in the titles listed under these headings in *Books for You: A Booklist for Senior High Students* prepared by Kenneth L. Donelson and the NCTE Committee on the Senior High School Booklist. They then list, classify, and analyze the various kinds of problems young people encounter and respond creatively to them. Different groups prepare volumes of "Spoon River Anthology" poetic monologues in which various characters discuss their problems, Dear Abby–Ann Landers letters and responses regarding problems, imaginative writing and artwork based on student problems, and a series of radio spot announcements, including lead-in music and brief dramatizations of problems and solutions.

5. Tenth graders exploring the values of television sitcoms work in groups, each group selecting a different series to view and interpret. After preparing a report of the values the series seems to promote and analyzing its basic features and design, each group prepares a script and produces either a satire or a serious program stressing those values and features.

6. Eleventh graders studying a particular period of literature and history prepare a series of newspapers with articles, news stories, editorials, and features based on events and publications of that period. As a model, they go to any Sunday supplement section of a newspaper, substituting articles appropriate for the period for the kind of articles in the original.

7. Twelfth graders in a humanities unit work in groups to select a period, an event, a humanistic concept, an artistic development, or a social innovation to explain, illustrate, document, and interpret in a multimedia presentation to be preserved and used with future classes. The teacher shows some Encyclopedia Britannica humanities films to suggest how the use of visuals and narration permits a slide-tape production.

Research Skills

The first emphasis on research skills should be to combat the common student belief that "research" means "library research" exclusively. On the contrary, students should be taught to begin with firsthand observation of the real world, to raise critical questions about their observations, to move to controlled manipulation of events and processes in the real world (experiments), and then to go to secondhand sources, such as interviews, surveys, and first-person reports, before going to printed materials, including those in libraries. This is not, of course, to minimize the importance of library work or to traduce the development of traditional library research skills; all are important.

1. Sixth graders, in connection with science study, conduct controlled experiments and record their observations. They are taught early to use the following general report form:
    (a) What bothered, disturbed, or challenged me (in short, why I did what I did or what I wanted to find out).
    (b) What I did.
    (c) What I observed.
    (d) What I concluded from what I observed.
    (e) What I shall do next, or what I recommend others do (if appropriate).

Experiments may range from noting germination times of seeds planted under various conditions, metamorphosis time of various cocoons, and incubation time of eggs, to effects of air pressure in collapsing evacuated cans, in holding paper covers tightly to inverted glasses of water, and in supporting tubes of mercury.

2. Seventh graders, introduced to the importance of usage and word choice in language, prepare a questionnaire including disputed and dialectal choices, and report on who in the community approves which items in which situations.

3. Eighth graders, in a unit on local government, make trips by appointment to city hall and the county courthouse. They talk with both elected and appointed officials and attorneys and prepare a list of information and services available from various offices, as well as obligations of citizens to such offices. (The teacher calls the local bar association to get help with arrangements.)

4. Ninth graders, in a unit on biography and collective biography, become interested in the Hall of Fame, the Nobel Prize, the Pulitzer Prize, the Drama Critics Circle Award, the National Book Award, and other honors for outstanding achievement. Working in groups, they prepare reports on the various honors; and as individuals, they prepare reports on outstanding honorees.

5. Tenth graders, having read or heard about such books as Samuel Butler's *Erewhon,* Edward Bellamy's *Looking Backward,* George Orwell's *1984,* and Aldous Huxley's *Brave New World,* read widely among the titles listed under "Utopias and Communes" in *Books for You: A Booklist for Senior High Students* prepared by Kenneth L. Donelson and the NCTE Committee on the Senior High School Booklist. They then do additional research on communes and utopias, research current thinking about the future, and prepare reports on their projections for the next century.

6. Eleventh graders, in a unit on "Contemporary American Culture," individually select aspects of American life in which they are interested (dance, art, city planning, transportation, sports). They research the area and write a chapter—both as a model of term paper form and as a survey of modern life—for "A Survey of Contemporary American Culture," a volume to be bound and contributed to the library reference shelf.

7. Twelfth graders participating in the kind of literature seminar described in Brooke Workman's *In Search of Ernest Hemingway* (Urbana: National Council of Teachers of English, 1979) proceed as a class through a series of reading and writing experiences which prepare them for individual research on a contemporary writer to be selected with the teacher's help. Workman recommends John Steinbeck and J. D. Salinger as more appealing to teenagers than F. Scott Fitzgerald and William Saroyan, and he specifically warns against such writers as William Faulkner, Henry James, and Saul Bellow because of length and difficulty of their works. Workman's method presumes uniform class experiences with a single writer, but the method is extendable to guided small-group or individual work.

A UNIT GROWS

Without presenting a fully developed unit, complete with performance objectives, long lists of highly desirable (but virtually unobtainable materials), and suggestions for evaluation procedures, it is nonetheless possible to suggest the way in which a teacher of the gifted takes a unit theme and works out a complete unit—with student help. Again, part of motivating students to do their best and providing them with opportunities to exercise their leadership and planning abilities requires that they be in on the development of a unit of study. The teacher will have in mind, of course, a number of both general and specific objectives based on an evaluation of the needs of the class, but many of these can be reached through a number of alternative means, the most effective of which may well be the means selected by students.

Here, then, is one teacher's emerging unit procedure in handling the theme "Life in the City."

Activities

1. The teacher plays a number of musical selections which

center on cities. Suggested are the following:

Bernstein, Leonard. *West Side Story*. The original sound track recording. Book by Arthur Laurents. Lyrics by Stephen Sondheim. Columbia Stereo CS2071. 2 s. 12″ 33⅓ rpm.

Copland, Aaron. *Quiet City*. Howard Hanson and the Eastman Rochester Orchestra. Mercury Stereo SR90421. 1 s. 12″ 33⅓ rpm.

Williams, Vaughan. *A London Symphony*. Sir John Barbirolli and The Hallé Orchestra. Angel Stereo S-36478. 2 s. 12″ 33⅓ rpm.

2. The teacher reads a number of poetic selections (or calls on outstanding student readers previously assigned to prepare and read dramatically). Suggestions are selections from the following works:

Adoff, Arnold, ed. *City in All Directions: An Anthology of Modern Poems*. New York: Macmillan, 1969.

Brooks, Gwendolyn. *Bronzeville Boys and Girls*. New York: Harper and Row, 1956.

Larrick, Nancy, ed. *On City Streets: An Anthology of Poetry*. New York: M. Evans and Company, 1968.

3. The teacher shows films or filmstrips or pictures which capture the flavor of the city or indicate the problems or future of the city. Suggested are the following:

The City, the Artist's View. New York: Sandak (4 East 48th Street, New York 10017). 25 frames, color, 35 mm. filmstrip.

1985. Crowell, Collier, and Macmillan. 56 min., color, 16mm. film.

2000 A. D. New York: Newsweek, 1973. Filmstrip.

23 Skidoo. New York: McGraw-Hill and Toronto: National Film Board of Canada. 8 min., black and white, 16 mm. film.

"Who Do You Kill?" and "No Hiding Place" from TV series "East Side, West Side." New York: Carousel Films (1501 Broadway, New York 10019). Both 50 min.

"Sense of the City." Limited free loan from CBS-TV. 28 min.

4. Students read extensively and individually in books listed in the following:

Cianciolo, Patricia, and the Committee on the Elementary School Booklist of the National Council of Teachers of English, *Adventuring with Books: A Booklist for Pre-K–Grade 8*. Urbana: National Council of Teachers of English, 1977. (Especially the sections on "Contemporary Life," "Ethnic Groups," and "Biography.")

Donelson, Kenneth L., and the Committee on the Senior High School Booklist of the National Council of Teachers of English, *Books for You: A Booklist for Senior High Students*. Urbana: National Council of Teachers of English, 1976. (Especially the sections on "Problems of Modern Humanity," "Collected Ethnic Experiences," "Urban Life, Urban Concerns," and "Utopias and Communes.")

5. Students read or listen to a number of high-interest short stories concerned with cities, city problems, and the future of cities. Possibilities might include the following:

Benet, Stephen Vincent, "By the Waters of Babylon"
Bradbury, Ray, "The Town Where No One Got Off" (in *Cities*, edited by Edith G. Stull)
Clark, Walter Van Tilburg, "The Portable Phonograph"
Gregory, Dick, "We Ain't Poor, Just Broke" (in *Nigger*)
Rosten, Leo, *The Education of H*y*m*a*n K*a*p*l*a*n* (most chapters)

6. Students listen to attorneys, community officials, or service club members who present their visions of the changing community and their hopes for the direction of change. If possible, they investigate any city planning documents for the future.

7. A small group explores the work of the local historical society, the available books and pamphlets on local history, and local history experts.

8. Small groups explore a number of books dealing with city planning and renewal, with theories of urban development, and with the sociology of the city. Recom-

mended are such volumes as the following:

Greeley, Andrew M. *Neighborhood.* New York: Seabury Press, 1977.

Hughes, Helen. *Cities and City Life.* Boston: Allyn and Bacon, 1970 (Sociological Resources for the Social Studies Series).

The Community, by the Editors of Time-Life Books. New York: Time-Life Books, 1976.

Fishman, Robert. *Urban Utopias in the Twentieth Century: Ebenezer Howard, Frank Lloyd Wright, Le-Corbusier, Robert Fishman.* New York: Basic Books, 1977.

Insel, Paul M. with Henry Clay Lindgren. *Too Close for Comfort: The Psychology of Crowding.* New Jersey: Prentice-Hall, 1978.

Mumford, Lewis. *My Works and Day.* New York: Harcourt, Brace, Jovanovich, 1979.

Lofland, Lyn H. *A World of Strangers: Order and Action in Urban Public Space.* New York: Basic Books, 1973.

Munzer, Martha E. and John Vogel, Jr. *New Towns: Building Cities from Scratch.* New York: Knopf, 1974. (Distributed by Random House)

Munzer, Martha E. *Planning Our Town.* New York: Knopf, 1964.

Stewart, Maxwell S. *Can We Save Our Cities? The Story of Urban Renewal.* New York: Public Affairs Committee, 1966.

Von Eckardt, Wolf. *Back to the Drawing Board: Planning Livable American Cities.* New York: New Republic, 1978.

Ward, Colin. *The Child in the City.* New York: Pantheon Books, 1978.

Weaver, Robert C. *Dilemmas of Urban America.* New York: Atheneum, 1967.

Wheeler, Thomas C. *A Vanishing America: The Life and Times of the Small Town* (Twelve Regional Towns). New York: Holt, Rinehart, and Winston, 1964.

9. Students participate in group discussions regarding cities. Well in advance of the scheduled discussion, stu-

dents work in a planning session during which time they list topics to investigate, questions to find information about, and problems to consider. Certain individuals and small groups volunteer to be responsible both for finding information and leading the discussion on certain areas. Students may suggest topics and questions such as these:

a. When did cities begin to emerge? Why did people congregate in cities? What needs do cities satisfy more easily than does rural life?

b. What services must cities provide in order to exist? In what ways has providing these services become more difficult recently? Why?

c. What values of rural or small-town life are sacrificed for large-city life?

d. What are some of the major "planned" cities of the world? What have their plans included? Why were they developed?

e. What are some of the "new towns" being developed in this century? How and why have they been created?

f. What new considerations should be provided for in future new towns?

g. How can existing towns be improved? What kinds of social and psychological considerations must supplement physical and architectural considerations?

h. How can education, recreation, culture, and entertainment be included in plans for cities?

10. Students take a field trip either to a big city or to selected places in the city in which they live. For example, few students in most large cities will have visited the city waterworks or sewage disposal plant. Few will have personal acquaintance with the various wholesale market areas. Few will have any idea of the operations of such offices as the sanitation department, the city planning department, the engineering department, or the traffic control office.

11. Students respond creatively to various aspects of city life. For example, after having seen "The Dehumanizing City . . . and Hymie Schultz" from the Searching for

Values Series, students write verse or stories about the frustration of the modern individual in conflict with complex bureaucratic systems. (A selection from the film *The Tiger Makes Out* with Eli Wallach, this film shows Hymie Schultz's futile attempt to fight back against bureaucracy. It is 15 minutes long, in color, available from Learning Corporation of America, 1973.)

12. Students examine zoning maps of their own city, consider implications of rezoning, and attempt to work out a better, more efficient, and more productive arrangement. Various students role-play different types of citizens whose homes, businesses, or interests are to be affected by the suggested rezoning.

13. Interested students research careers in city management, politics, and city planning. They attempt to procure speakers knowledgeable in these areas.

14. Students participate in debates on various subjects. Each participant must prepare in advance a "brief" of the main points of the argument to be presented. Topics include such propositions as the following:
    a. Life in the city is more rewarding than life in the small town or country.
    b. City planning is preferable to haphazard, laissez-faire growth.
    c. The right of eminent domain (the law permitting governments to preempt private property for public good) should be extended to include all aspects of the public good, including recreation, aesthetics, etc.
    d. Voluntary self-segregation in neighborhoods according to ethnic or religious background, race, and socioeconomic level is inevitable and constructive.

15. Students write letters to chambers of commerce in various cities requesting information regarding developments which have recently improved life in the cities and brochures regarding recreational and social opportunities in the cities.

Evaluation

Evaluation will again be based on personal, peer, and teacher judgment of the effort, depth, and value of each individual student's production. As before, students will write out a self-evaluation, referring specifically to research, reports, and written work, while peers independently write out evaluations of the same materials. The teacher then prepares final individual evaluations, communicating them, when possible, to students in individual conferences.

THE GIFTED STUDENT AND THE "BASIC SKILLS"

Though most teachers of the gifted would argue that the "basic skills" are accurate perception, logical processing of information, and confident creativity—or some such roster of higher-level skills—the fact is that state assessment and the back-to-the-basic movement have convinced the public that the *basics* are "really" low-level reading comprehension, spelling, capitalization, punctuation, usage, manuscript and letter form, and basic arithmetic. These are the skills measured on most "competency" tests.

Since this entire publication is concerned with the higher-level skills which most teachers of the gifted would consider basic, perhaps it is in order to give some attention to the "basics" as they are popularly understood. What about gifted students and such low-level language arts skills as minimal reading comprehension, spelling, capitalization, punctuation, usage, and manuscript and letter form?

Parents, administrators, and school patrons have a right to expect that the gifted—as well as all other students—be well grounded in these basics. Unfortunately, teachers of the gifted—who a generation ago might have assumed that their students have already mastered these skills—cannot now do so! The reason is *not* that students or education is worse than twenty years ago, but rather that two factors are operating: (1) the total culture today provides fewer opportunities for experience with precision and depth in reading and writing and fewer rewards for achievement in those areas, and (2) there is growing recognition that virtually no one "masters" these areas at an early age so as to be forever after free of need to focus on them. Some people were shocked when the National Assessment of Educational Progress disclosed that students in the upper grades seem to have as many problems with usage and mechanics as those in the lower grades! But National Council of Teachers of English Associate Executive Secretary John Maxwell believes that the continuation of such errors is inevitable. As students write more maturely, address themselves to more complex concerns, and experiment with more sophisticated linguistic forms, they will naturally err from time to time. It is a part of the natural, inevitable growth and learning process.

Nonetheless, teachers of the gifted neither must accept sloppy work on basic skills as inevitable, nor must they be stampeded into overkill in an attempt through direct attack and drill to eradicate unacceptable forms and inculcate standard ones. Indeed, either course would be disastrous.

Mechanics are important for the acceptance of a communication and for the credibility of the communicator. If the gifted are to lead in the future, they must certainly acquire the skills which gain them acceptance.

On the other hand, there is ample evidence to indicate that the gifted will not be confined to basic drills and that the surest way to destroy their respect both for the basics we wish to promote and the schooling we represent is to keep them too long on too low a level.

There is evidence also that as students are actively involved in purposeful communication and as they receive the natural feedback which purposeful communication generates, their communications are, in large part, self-correcting and their skills self-improving. The teacher's role is to represent the mass of largely conservative American "consumers of language" and to remind students constantly of the importance for credibility of standard edited English, occasionally to help with forms and distinctions, and frequently to provide interesting, enlightening, and active experience when necessary. Occasional drills are perfectly acceptable—but only when they are short, purposeful, interesting, and social—rather than long, useless, boring, and lonely. The gifted should be taught to be investigators and observers of language and sent often both to specialized volumes for information and to the marketplace for observation. As they become interested in and concerned with language, they will teach themselves.

References

1. Apple, Natalie. "A Study of the Literature Objectives of the Pittsburgh Scholars Program in English, Grades 10 and 11." Doctoral dissertation, University of Pittsburgh, 1979.
2. Dewey, John. *School and Society.* Chicago: University of Chicago Press, 1899.
3. Gallagher, James J. "Research Summary on Gifted Child Education." Monograph. State of Illinois, Office of Superintendent of Public Instruction, 1966.
4. Gavin, William F. "The Faculty Club, Wittenberg." *English Journal* 56, no. 1 (January 1967) :37.
5. Guilford, J. P. "The Structure of the Intellect." *Psychological Bulletin* 53 (1956) :267–93.
6. Tierney, Patricia. "A Study of the Composition Objectives of the Pittsburgh Scholars Program in English, Grades 10 and 11." Doctoral dissertation, University of Pittsburgh, 1979.
7. Tuttle, Frederick B., Jr., and Becker, Laurence A. *Program Design and Development for Gifted and Talented Students.* Washington, D.C.: National Education Association, 1980.